Insights From Life

A Poetic Voyage to Inner Space

By Steven Lawrence Getz

Dedications

These poems are for Gloria F. Getz. She encouraged me to
write them.

About the Author

Steven L. Getz composes poems from the emotions of personal experience, as well as the emotions of personal experiences he observed in the lives of others. He had a bent, but basically happy, childhood, followed by an awkward lingering adolescence and tenuous adulthood. Like many people, he seeks simplicity, then distrusts it. Words flow from him like water.

Table of Contents

Author's Fore-blurb

In my poems you will find

Introspections from a worldly mind.

Some are pensive, some are kind,

But they helped me pass my time,

I hope that you'll enjoy my wit,

And don't consider me a twit.

By the time that your read this book all through,

You'll find that I am very much like you.

In my poems, you will see

Life's dominant personalities.

As words poured freely from my mind,

These personalities slowly were defined.

Some thoughts are flippant, and some are tender,

Some are distant, but still rendered.

Most are harmless, but some are lethal,

And some were borrowed from other people.

Some poems are passionate, yet filled with strife

And though not pretty, they're part of life.

Some will leave you open-eyed.

So, buckle up for a sentient ride.

Book Section on Ponderings

Ponderings

Does a broken mirror reflect again?

Are we shadowed by our past and sins?

Can fallen flowers return to branches?

Are our traumas rippling avalanches?

Is fate a tightrope we must follow?

Can we control our chain of morrows?

Is our past a ball and chain we drag?

Is it a burden or a flag?

What is faith and what is soul?

Do they restrain our lives and goals?

What is God? Is He near?

Does He even know we're here?

Why do these questions cloud our mind?

Are they common to man and womankind?

Deus Ex Machina?

Like Job, I've known what is right and wrong,

And I try to take the view that is long.

Though I'm not perfect, I do fear God,

(Which, in modern times, does seem odd).

But *what is God*, I ask you now?

A burning bush? A sacred cow?

Or is God simply an advanced being,

Who *seems* all-knowing and all-seeing?

If God sees everything everywhere,

Am I important?--Does He care?

Is my lifeline some script I follow

In His program filled with joys and sorrows?

If so, are all my tribulations

Simply His computer simulations?

Though these thoughts make me weary,

They keep me guessing and God-fearing.

"Deus ex machina" is a Latin translation of

an ancient Greek phrase that described the

way masked actors who represented deities

appeared during theatrical plays held in ancient Greece. These deities usually remained on an elevated platform that was hidden from the general audience during the first two acts of the play. Once the play's plot reached its final climax (usually during the third act), these actors representing deities were lowered down from their hidden heavenly perch by ropes and pulleys to the stage below so that they could sort out the complex problems that had developed among 'mere mortals' that lived on the earth's surface.

Wanderlust Winds

Souls borne on wanderlust winds

Never their wandering fate rescind.

They wander like winds throughout their lives

Enslaved to adventure for which they strive.

Living life on its razor-thin edge

At the tip of fate's precarious wedge,

They ride like Valkyries into war,

Not knowing what life is really for.

Some are heroes, and some are rogues

Who will constantly wring from life its most.

But, in the end, they are lusty slaves

To their itchy feet's whims

And life's wondrous ways.

Life Sentence on Death Row

Back and forth the monkey paces

Alone is his small backyard cage.

He did not make his cramped cage,

But the small cage makes him.

Far away, he sees children in a park

Running free and laughing.

He also sees birds flying free

And singing far from his small cage.

But in his barred cramped world,

He can only take short paces

Then swing rhythmically back and forth,

Back and forth, among the bars,

From day to day and year to year.

The monkey does not laugh or sing,

And no one plays with him.

Long ago, when he was young,

He ran free in a jungle with his brothers.

But now, he only takes short paces

Then swings back and forth,

And back and forth,

Waiting for a solitary death

That may not come for years.

Vortex of Thought

Within the gyre of life self-centered,

Spins mental debris long since splintered.

This maelstrom of memories stretches and

lengthens until a breaking point is reckoned.

Do bad dreams, and sins forgotten,

Lurk in minds long roiled and rotten?

And where's our relief from nocuous

Nightmares,

Vexing romances, and unanswered prayers?

When does the circle of life bring closure,

And will it end in full disclosure?

Life is too short for questions long

And it should not end like a tragic song.

Alone at the Top

He always endeavored to win alone

And over the years, his methods he honed.

He projected strength and never seemed evil,

But others (to him) were throw-away people.

Most were people he barely knew,

And some were souls whose use was through.

A few were kinfolk that he knew well.

But in the end, they also fell.

People resented his wiles and ways

That he achieved his selfish goals each day.

He lied, cheated, and encroached upon rights,

So that he could win his impossible fights.

Lives were destroyed and futures were lost,

Leaving many with deep emotional costs.

But now he's alone after merciless toils,

With no one to love and share his spoils.

He is an ostracized soul who won alone,

Now emptily reaping what he has sown.

The Four Horsemen

The first one rode a white horse

And carried a sword and hunter's bow.

He seized the mantle of Man by force,

Then conquered all that I know.

The next one rode a roan horse

And carried a warrior's sword.

He shouted battle cries 'till hoarse

And killed thousands in civil wars.

Then third man came on a black horse

With a sword and scales at hand.

He brought justice and gave our farmers voice

When famine wracked our land.

Next came a man on an ashen horse

From Hades who smelled of death.

Hunger and pestilence soon arrived in force

And stayed 'till the birth of Seth.

The four horsemen of life's apocalypses

Always arrive one by one.

They feed on society's relationships

And wreak havoc till days are done.

Do Souls Dream?

Is death a dimension of misplaced minds

That we, as humans, cannot fathom?

When our bodies die, will we find

An existence entirely unimagined?

Are souls of the dead elated in eternity?

Do they bask in Heaven's warmth and mirth?

Or do they look back nostalgically,

And ponder their former stay(s) on earth?

As souls drift down eternity's stream,

Do they remain pious and devout?

When people die, do their souls dream?

And, if souls do, what do they dream about?

Different Perspectives

There are those who think with their head

From the time they're born until dead.

For them, things always seem logical.

Sometimes profound, but never magical.

And there are those who think with their heart,

Who are living in a world quite apart.

They wear their hearts on their sleeves low

And end up like Venus de Milo.

Most people straddle the fence

In order to ensure life makes sense.

They spend their precarious days

Avoiding heads and hearts from both ways.

Communist Leaders Contemplating Violent Actions in Tiananmen Square

Are we so blind

We cannot see.

We've met the enemy

And they are we.

Still Waters Run Deep

Waters still and waters deep,

Always will their secrets keep.

Life is short and memories long,

Yet every life still sings its song.

The Other Side of Silence

There's another side of silence,

Which no one ever hears.

It is rarely ever absent,

And it often raises fears.

We sometimes feel its presence

While we're far from home

And cultivate its essence

When we are alone.

In it are some lessons,

Which we should try to learn.

It's steeped in our obsessions,

And it causes wheels to turn.

This other side of silence

Is our hidden self.

We look to it for guidance,

For in it wisdom dwells.

The Colored Lens of Life

Things taught black and things taught white

When I was young and caged,

Became a brilliant-colored quilt

When teens rushed through my age.

Things swarmed shadowed shades of gray

Once I turned middle-aged,

Then circled back to black and white

As I became a sage.

The Lonely Lie

Once there was a lonely lie

That crawled off by itself to die.

But, before it even left the room,

Its offspring had begun to bloom.

Soon the truth had lost its place

And it quietly left in sad disgrace.

It's crowded now in that small room

And honor there you can't presume.

The Rainy Soul

One day while waiting for my train,

I saw a woman standing in pouring rain.

Rain rolled from her umbrella freely

And splashed down on the platform near me.

Her saddened eyes looked very teary,

As though contemplating something eerie.

She was a mannequin dressed in dour despair

And said no words while standing there.

But once the New York train arrived,

She stepped aboard and looked alive.

Not looking back, she took her seat,

As though some new life she would meet.

Her distant stare into parts unknown,

Upon my memory has slowly grown.

But I've often wondered what she was thinking

While her rain-drenched soul was sinking.

View from the Cult

I gave them all my riches,

I gave them all my fame,

I gave them all the things I loved

That caused me woe and shame.

Now I sit here penniless,

With no one else to blame,

Attempting to achieve some happiness,

In a cult that numbed my name.

I am now a swollen vessel,

Turgid with cult beliefs,

A homeless penniless vassal,

Who depends on his cult to eat.

Others wonder why I've done

The things that changed my life.

But I knew my ego must be shunned

Because it only brought me strife.

The cult accepted me, a troubled youth,

Who was Hell-bent on destruction.

But they also knew I challenged truths,

And society's specious deceptions.

At the banks of my mental Rubicon,

I elected to take the plunge,

Knowing my cast die tumbled on

A past I could not expunge.

Others made the plunge with me.

They too, took the risk.

They too, wanted to be free

Of society's smothering fist.

Now we are all on hostile ground,

In a society that we have shaken.

But, to our cult, we are now bound,

And we realize the risks that we've taken.

We no longer drift like icebergs,

In some cold conscious conformity.

Portions of our egos have been purged,

Which masked our id's enormity.

Mind Chatter

Its noisy din in silent rooms

Leaves orphaned thoughts and focus doomed.

Its silent clatter seems so loud

That thoughts get lost in its clamorous clouds.

It melts your mind and drowns your dreams

While thoughts inside you weakly scream.

You dream each day to free your mind

From chatter's clatter, unconfined.

Debt

An irksome thing that nags your mind

And strangles hope until you're blind.

You own it now; it owns you next.

It drains your dreams until you're vexed.

Your life becomes a moneyed wreck,

From sleepless nights filled full of frets.

It draws you down into its flood,

And bleeds your soul while you weep blood.

Your anxiety grows until you scream,

"ENOUGH, ENOUGH, GIVE BACK MY

DREAMS!"

Snow Has No Voice

Snow has no voice,

But thunders when it moves

Down a rugged mountainside

Following its contoured groves.

Avalanches of emotion

Consume all in their path,

And kindness and devotion

Are destroyed by their wrath.

Dark Visitor

Death came to my room one day.

Gravely ill, I was his prey.

He watched for a while but could not stay.

So, silently, he backed away.

Role Models

The human canvas is very broad

And painted with many people,

So, there is nothing really odd

About meeting ones deceitful.

But sometimes a person comes into view,

Who heralds the best of humanity.

And before that day is through,

They vanquish all your vanity.

They give you all they have,

Expecting nothing in return,

And their honest, simple laugh,

Makes your conscience burn.

Once you let them into your life,

Things never seem to worsen.

They slowly end your daily strife

And make you a better person.

Parallel Lives

Parallel lives sometimes merge

And change their track forever,

But staggered lives and tandem lives

May not cross each other ever.

Once two parallel lives merge,

Their changes can be dramatic

As they experience love and death,

On the wings of fate's wild antics.

They become droplets moving down life's glass,

That bond and then grow larger.

But, if other droplets on that glass

Don't merge, they will stay smaller.

Is God so capricious that

He separates our fates,

So that He can weave our lives together

Before it is not too late?

Eyes of Despair

From rumpled bags of abject rags

Cast off along life's road,

Came cryptic stares and unsaid dares,

That judged my labored load.

No festive themes or rainbowed dreams

I saw in those stark stares,

Just saddened schemes and silent screams

That lurked in languid lairs.

Walking past her bags and abject rags,

I finally chanced to ask,

"What in your wan life have you done,

To make your life so taxed?"

"I was uncouth throughout my youth,"

She said with no great flair.

"My soul got snagged, and I got dragged,

Into a vortex of dour despair.

"If you could save just one poor knave,

From your sad fate," I asked,

"What would you say to those who'd stray,

From virtue when they're tasked?"

"Do not get shunned and die undone.

Good morals you must adopt.

"Or, you'll be like me, life's sad debris."

She said as her tearful eyes dropped.

The Well

As a child, I found a well,

In a large grassy meadow.

And I clambered up its rocky sides

So that its secrets I would know.

On that day, I had no thirst,

Merely a child-like curiosity.

Its walls were rough and very steep,

And its bottom I could not see.

Looking around, a stone I found,

And tossed it down the well.

Then I listened for a sound,

To judge how far it fell.

After what seemed a lengthy time,

I heard a muted thud,

Which told me that either the well was dry

Or filled with thick dry mud.

People are dark deep wells

With depths you'll never know,

And have thoughts you can't perceive

When words at them you throw.

Not as Separate Islands

We live not as separate islands,

In an endless human ocean.

And we must try to understand

We are ruled by our emotions.

When we express our gratitude,

It changes countless other lives.

And in the end, our attitude

Reflects that for which we strive.

No matter what the prejudiced say,

Think or have suggested,

In many strange and cryptic ways,

Our souls are all connected.

Porcelain Doll

She was a porcelain doll

From a French-Spanish womb

And had a Basque drawl

That drew men to her room.

With eyes colored green,

She attracted most men,

And her bisque-colored sheen

Was popular with them.

But, behind her pale mask,

Was a childhood so cruel

That her kinfolk from Basque

Knew that she was no jewel.

Though her looks were stunning,

She lacked all propriety.

But her good looks and cunning,

Helped her rise in society.

She climbed very high,

And she moved very fast.

Yet, no one decried

Her mysterious past.

Eventually, she finally fell

When her false front was shattered.

There were no romantic farewells

And her suitors soon scattered.

Cored by a Tinge of Blue

Remember where you came from

And what you had to do

To achieve your present outcome

Before your life was through.

Your life has reached duality.

Rumor is now the known,

And your stereotyped personality

Has assumed a life of its own.

Now that you are famous

Your private life is through,

Your flame of fame is flickering

But it's cored by a tinge of blue.

Fly on the Wall

I wish that I could be

A fly on the wall,

Who watches, hears and sees,

But is not noticed at all.

Armed with what I hear and see,

Learned, and understand,

Liars would never feel at ease.

Wouldn't that be grand?

Never a Wasted Life

There has never been a wasted life,

The evidence for this is ample.

For, even if you fail in all you do,

You can be used as a bad example.

He Was a Young Man Once

He was a young man once

Who wore a young man's clothes.

He accomplished things with brilliance,

Though now, few people know.

He lived with proud panache,

And loved with a heart so true,

That winsome women he romanced

Wished they were never through.

But he is an old man now

Who wears an old man's clothes.

Though once proud in his prime,

Few people, if any, know.

Table Grace

Thank you, Lord, for simple things

That family life unto us brings.

Our family bonds bind us all

While worlds around us rise and fall.

Our children are our family's hope,

They teach us how to love and cope.

Please keep our children free of stress

And imbue their hearts with happiness.

Things you provide our joy ensures

And enable our family to endure.

You help our humble hearts to sing.

Thank you, Lord, for everything.

They Say

They say to love your enemies

And turn your other cheek.

But then, they tease you with great glee

And beat you until you are weak.

They say to love the meek,

For they'll inherit earth.

But many ignore the meek

And claim they have no worth.

They say it's blessed to give to others

while expecting nothing in return.

But most people expect to be repaid,

That you quickly learn.

They say God loves bad people too

And he does not take sides.

But most believe the pious ones

Get God's easiest ride.

They say that pride's an awful sin

That one should always avoid.

But pride is how most gauge their worth,

And without it, life's a void.

They say that money has evil's roots,

And happiness it cannot buy.

But people get angry once it's gone.

And, for it, many die.

Many of the things religion teaches

May be too ideal.

So, people don't always adhere to them

Because they're too ideal.

My Hedonistic Brother

My younger brother lived for now,

But never for the when.

He danced and drank his life away,

Again, again, and again.

I reminded him how both ants and squirrels

Saved food for wintery times.

But he only laughed and partied more

And prayed for warmer climes.

I warned him I would not carry him

Once his spending money was gone.

But he simply stared at me silently,

Then laughed and partied on.

Upon turning fifty, he ran out of cash,

But never out of arrogance.

Instead, he married an elderly spinster,

Who died leaving him an inheritance.

He lives now in a home I can't afford

And drives a new Rolls Royce.

He throws the wildest parties in town

And lives his daily life by choice.

I wanted to shake my fist into the sky,

And bellow, "WHERE'S THE FAIRNESS!"

But I was so glad to be free of him,

I simply went about my business.

There Are None

There is none who is so blind,

Than those who will not see.

There are none who are so bound

Than those who can't be free.

There are none who are so deaf

Than those who will not listen.

There are none who are so dull

Than those who never glisten.

There are none who are so mute

Than those who will not speak.

There are none who are so bad

Than those who torture the meek.

There are none who are so hard

Than those who've been mistreated.

There is none who is so vexed

Than those who have been cheated.

Who Cries For the Orphans?

Who cries for the orphans,

So scared and so alone,

Without a caring parent,

To comfort them at home?

Who cries for the lovers,

Who've lost the ones they loved,

Obsessed by grief-filled misery,

Without their mate beloved?

Who cries for the soldiers,

Who die so far from home,

Bleeding on a distant battlefield,

Where both the brave and fearful roam?

Are these souls abandoned,

Alone, ignored, and unblessed?

Or does God simply carry them,

While their faith he tests?

Live in the Light

Turn the eye of your soul toward light,

Do not in darkness dwell.

Let your happiness exude might,

Do not sad stories tell.

Wear not your heart on your sleeve,

But don't hide it where none can see.

Learn to laugh, love and grieve,

And let your imagination run free.

Bask in youth's light while there,

Don't despair in your place or lot.

But know that life begs flair,

For, an unexamined life lives not.

Try to move toward the Lord's light,

Don't dwell in your dark shadows behind.

Dance in the twilight until it is night,

For darkness and guilt aren't kind.

From Dream to Dream

We move in life from dream to dream.

But are our lives what they seem?

What about our loves and hates?

Do they turn on luck or life's mistakes?

Does God or nature control our thoughts?

Does chance control what life has wrought?

Or does all and every decision we make

Depend on tactics that others take?

Are lives, loves, and acts in kind

Simply ruses hatched in other's minds.

Let's hope our dreams are what they seem,

And not merely schemes in others' dreams.

Memories

Some are printed vividly

Upon our waking minds.

Some are muddied purposely

And remain poorly defined.

Some remain our treasures

Like fondest childhood times.

Some suffer quick erasure

And are not so sublime.

Some are clumped together

Like piles of videotape.

Some are broken feathers

From which we can't escape.

Our memories often slowly merge,

As they are fused by time.

And, though they often ebb and surge,

They always seem to rhyme.

As we slowly live our lives,

We will gradually all see

How fate's threads control our lives

And connect our memories.

Life's Echoes

Memories are life's echoes

That reverberate through our minds,

Then melt away like Spring snows

In cerebral sites confined.

Some we treasure all our life,

But others we can't forget,

Because they arise from past strife,

And situations that made us fret.

In our thoughts, bad memories dwell,

Unless they're laid to rest.

But haunting thoughts we cannot quell,

Will always leave us stressed.

Mellow lives are usually blessed

By many pleasant memories

That mirror a lifetime with no stress

And keep their souls at ease.

Book Section on Love and Consequences

Love Is a Oneness of Two

Love is a oneness of two

In the things that you say and do.

Love quells troubles and strife

And helps with your struggles in life.

Love comes from within not without.

And once it's there, there's never a doubt.

To surrender to love, you must go

To a future that you do not yet know.

To be loved is something we need,

Without it, our souls can never be freed.

Love's power makes other things last.

Its dimensions are truly vast.

Love comes from tenderness and care.

Once it's gone, you enter despair.

Walled in by loneliness,

You pine for the oneness

Of two that you left behind.

Three Little Words

Three little words 'I love you'

Can be difficult to say

But carry so much meaning,

That we need them every day.

Without them we become lost

As we wind our ways through days,

Their worth exceeds their cost

In so many different ways.

The simple words 'I love you',

That we often fail to say

Affects all of our relationships

Throughout life's weary way.

Money can bring you freedom,

And talent can bring you fame,

But love defines the kingdom,

Contained within God's name.

You Are Out There

I don't know what you look like,

I do not know your name.

But when I finally meet you,

I'll never be the same.

Right now, my spirit's soaring,

As fate moves me toward you.

You'll be so adoring,

And that will set me free.

You do not know what I look like,

You do not know my name.

But once that you have met me,

You'll never be the same.

Your spirit's also soaring

As fate moves you to me.

I will be so adoring

And that will set you free.

I know that you'll embrace me,

You'll treat me right I know.

I know that you will love me,

And our love will always grow.

We are waiting for one another,

Hoping to come together.

We're longing to love one another,

And hoping our love lasts forever.

We are both still out there,

And right now, we're alone.

Yet we are a matched pair,

Of fate's dice not thrown.

In the Stillness of the Hours

Deep within the night

In the stillness of the hours

Her spirit slowly comes to me

Like the fragrance of Spring flowers.

Silently, she soothes my sorrows

And I strive to keep her near

So that the bothers of the morrow

Will not flood my soul with fear.

Throughout the night she comforts me

As she cures my forlorn heart

With her happiness and passion sweet,

Before the night departs.

Noiselessly, the night moves on,

And with the dawn of day,

She strokes my soul one final time

Then slowly steals away.

Love Will Light Their Way

When you think that all is lost,

And there's nothing more to say,

Look back upon the lines you crossed,

The ones from which you strayed.

Could you have said things differently,

Or been more loving and gentile?

For, it is not always what you say,

But how your words make others feel.

Once you have lost benevolence,

To others, you are soon known

As that selfish person across life's fence

Who laughs and wins alone.

Life is not a game of chess,

With throw-away people to move.

It's a roller coaster filled with stress,

Tracked by grace, respect, and love.

When you treat people with respect,

And you help them every day,

They will come back to with you,

And love will light their way.

Opening a Hard Heart's Door

Love is not a weakness,

It is the glue that binds us all,

And when passion voids its presence,

Relationships soon fall.

Hearts are merely gardens

That allow love's seeds to grow,

And kindness unlocks a hard heart's door

More than prideful people know.

Pride can be useful,

But not in love's domain,

Though love gives hearts sunshine,

Pride drowns them with rain.

The simple words "I love you,"

Proffered when not asked for,

Do far more than any flowery written words

To open a hard heart's door.

Circling the Flame

The fickle, flickering flame

Danced wildly in the breeze.

Ever so closer she came

Until its bright light warmed her knees.

Slowly she circled the flame

Doing her dance with death.

Ever so closer she came

Until she was singed,

by the flame's hot breath.

She backed away wildly beguiled

Then gave it a perplexed stare.

To be deceived by something so wild

Was more than her soul could bear.

But the flame would not be denied.

It beckoned her back with its dancing light.

Consumed by emotion she sighed

Then flew 'round the bright light in the night.

Eventually she circled too close

And was burnt by the hot lusty flame.

Now consumed by love's overdose,

She knew that she had lost love's game.

As she fluttered and fell to earth dying,

The flame started beckoning another.

The candle of love is alluring.

But, for it, there will always be others.

Papillon

Women called him '*Papillon*',

And many knew him well.

He always pursued young naïve girls

Who he knew would not kiss and tell.

Many slept with him when they were younger,

But now they were as old as him,

Watching him flit to opening flowers

After he had deflowered them.

They knew he had 'basket eyes'

And loved young naive girls.

And most were not surprised

When dark clouds around him began to swirl.

Eventually, he seeded the underaged daughter

Of a man hard-nosed and prim,

And was forced to seek shelter at a wedding alter

When matron ravens tried to devour him.

I Love You and I Hate You

I love you, and I hate you

And don't know why I do.

I don't know how to leave you,

I'm confused through and through.

You light me like a torch,

Until my soul you scorch.

I hope you do not stay.

But never go away.

I have become two different lovers

With you beneath the covers.

I don't know what to do.

I hope we're never through.

The Unanswered Phone

You should have loved me

As much as I loved you.

You should have kissed me

The way that I kissed you.

You should have respected me

With the respect that I have for you.

You should have been faithful to me,

As I always was with you.

You should have talked to me those days

When I cried and begged you to.

You should have asked me to stay

When I left and said we're through.

<u>But you did not</u>.

So, the phone rings on and on.

And I ignore it without a thought.

Because, for you, I'll always be gone.

Three Questions

I asked her why she went with him

And she did not respond.

But I saw emotions skip across her face

Like thrown stones skittering on a pond.

I asked her if she loved him,

And knew what she was doing.

But that only seemed to strain chances

Of our relationship renewing.

So, I asked her, "If you were I,

What would you now do?"

Then, she turned and walked away

As though she had nothing more to lose.

When I love a woman

When I love a woman,

My cup of life spills over.

But, when I lose that woman,

I feel my life is over.

My heart becomes a shadow,

Cast upon a cold and empty room.

And, like a bud that cannot grow,

It just shrivels away un-bloomed.

Love seems so short,

And forgetting seems so long.

Her scent, her smile, her heart,

Once familiar, now are gone.

I try, but can't forget her,

And my days have a sluggish start,

Until I meet another woman,

Whose love can fill my heart.

There are secrets in life's shadows,

And secrets within our souls,

Things that we never really know,

Until love makes us whole.

Bedroom Eyes

Dark mischievous bedroom eyes

Are laden with lust and laden with lies.

They slowly cause my pulse to rise

And always do me hypnotize.

They exude passion's lusty flame,

The flame that sears, the flame that maims,

While masking their sinful secretive lies,

Behind a seductive sexual prize.

Should I stay, or should I leave?

I muse while my heart rides on my sleeve.

Such eyes have caused the death of innocence.

And, as for love, they have no relevance.

So, I back away from those sinful eyes,

So laden with lust, so laden with lies.

Because bedroom eyes are pools too deep,

And always will their secrets keep.

Mad, Bad, and Dangerous to Know

I met her in more turbulent times

While wandering to-and-fro.

I was no longer in my prime

And my heart had room to grow.

Our hurried romance left me beguiled

And vulnerable to her advances.

But like a motherless newborn child,

I had few, if any, chances.

I cast my lot with hers and hoped

Her languid love for me would grow.

But her witchy ways just left me duped,

And made me mad, bad, and dangerous to know.

A Soul Adrift

Drifting, drifting, drifting,

Through my life, I'm sifting,

For times that bring you nigh,

And cause my heart to sigh.

Good times we held so dear,

Are memories I keep nearby.

I miss those times of joy,

They make my sad heart buoy.

In those times, I retreat,

So once more I can meet,

The best half of my heart,

Your death has ripped apart.

Like a ship untethered,

I'm no longer anchored,

My broken heart is rifting,

While my sad soul is drifting.

December Dusk

Wintery winds and flurried evenings

Wear me down and raise dark doubts,

About my life without your loving,

I feel so lonely, down, and out.

Blustery days still chill my body,

The one you warmed so well in bed.

I'm still alive, but oh so lonely,

Though my heart beats, I feel dead.

I should have begged for your forgiveness

When you left while we were young,

Before long years imbued with emptiness

Framed the void where my soul's hung.

The many decades since I saw you

Wail like winds against life's wall.

I never dreamed that we'd be through,

I thought that love could conquer all.

When I hold your faded photo

In my shaking hands, I see

The face that still makes my heart glow

In this cold deep wintery freeze.

I know now you're gone forever

and forever can be very cruel.

Hearts can burn and often sever

When pride becomes their only fuel.

Staring at the blue-tinged snow

In dusk's feint disappearing light,

I long for the past sensuous times

That filled our many long love-filled nights.

I still use the love that you gave me

To slake the thirst of my dry soul.

I need your lips pressed to my body,

Those tender lips that kept me whole.

Though those memories fade in twilight,

I still cling tight to things you said.

Your pillowed words with gentle insight

That I'll cherish until I am dead.

The Younger Wife

After ten years of marriage, he cast me aside,

For a younger woman with bounce in her stride.

He said that he loved her,

And she made him feel young.

Then he said I was dated and too overstrung.

So, I looked in my mirror to see what he saw

And I saw an old woman

Whose emotions were raw.

Age took its toll and wrinkles don't lie,

What I saw in my mirror made my soul cry.

By chance, two years later, we met on the street.

He seemed evasive, and our eyes did not meet.

But I just kept on looking to learn how he fared.

(I still had fond memories of decades we shared.)

"Can we talk?" I said, when our eyes finally met.

"I hope you're now happy and have no regrets."

He thought for a moment, then looked far way,

I could tell from his look he had nothing to say.

Grasses are seductive on the wild side of fences,

And failed relationships lack recompenses.

Old stallions think wild grasses taste best,

But they often find them hard to digest.

Tables Turned

We met in spring when flowers bloomed

After several winter months cocooned.

At first, we were only casual lovers,

But became two halves made for each other.

Her looks, her sounds, her shape, her smell,

Seemed just right for me as I could tell.

But was she the One, that Soul-Mate One,

Who would change my life for years to come?

****

In July, our passion grew intense.

Love spiraled on and made good sense.

We seemed as one—but still were two,

Our love, it seemed, would never be through.

My friends all said, "Hey, she's the One.

Close the deal! Her heart you've won!"

But then, the Dogs of Doubt appeared."

Is something missing here?" I feared.

Was it missing in her? Was it missing in me?

Was it missing in us? Why could I not see?

Would it surface later, on life's long stage?

Would our love grow greater, or fade with age?

****

As September cooled love's fatuous flames,

I began my womanizing games.

My basket-eyed vile vagrancies,

Sourced her jaundiced jealousies.

Soon, I learned the terrible cost

Of killing romance's albatross.

Nothing is worse than a woman spurned,

And once they're spurned, they twist and burn.

Soon, her spirit seemed remote,

And her spite upon my soul she wrote.

Like me, she strayed, but like a cat,

She came back home in times not fat.

She'd lost my love but won it back.

I judged the cost, and then I packed.

I left her, <u>but back I came,</u>

I missed her cleft; she fanned lust's flame.

Once more I left, but soon returned.

She was too deft, for her I burned,

And burned and burned and burned.

Soon, my friends became concerned.

"Leave her now," they chimed in chorus.

"She's bad for you, and hence for us.

She's trapped you in her witchy spell

And made your life a living Hell!"

Said I, "Too late, she's seized my soul."

My heart is paying cheating's toll.

She's trapped me in her witchy game,

My heart's too thin, my spirit's too lame.

I'm racked with rage on love's wild ride,

I'll never save my crippled pride.

I know my life, and know her well,

I caused this strife, I'm in her spell."

Soon love's bank was overdrawn,

Deposits were needed for love to spawn.

Would she return my love for fashion?

Or would she ignore my poignant passion?

My die was tumbling, she gripped hers close,

My life was crumbling, I felt morose.

Could I lure her back to love's warm fold?

Or would I languish in Limbo's cold?

****

At winter's height, my money ended,

My soul fell flat, now undefended.

I'd doubted love and paid love's toll.

So, she dug her claws into my soul.

She left me flat and so alone

My life became a mindless moan.

She'd taken all, and left me weeping

With hard stale bread and faucets leaking.

After she left, single life was rough,

Other women simply weren't enough.

I needed love's cruel respite,

And hungered for her vixen bite.

****

One year later, I could see,

The one I missed the most was me.

The former me-the happy me,

The one who loved and laughed with glee.

It's been a year, but I still look,

For her fair face in each crowd's nook.

And I ask myself at each day's end, "

Can my lovers be my friends?"

Parting of Soul Mates

Don't leave, I still love you,

I know that we're not through.

For love, we have both cried,

Our rift is not that wide.

Wait now, you must not go.

Don't leave, I love you so.

What words can I now say

To make you stop and stay?

Think twice before you leave.

When gone, for you I'll grieve.

The pain my soul now feels,

Shows my need for you is real.

You're gone now, my life is vexed.

I'm alone, sad and perplexed.

My light is left on for you,

And it helps me see this through.

I'll watch for your return

While my poor heart burns.

I'll wait 'til time is done,

Though two, we should be one.

The Other Man

I've tried very hard to make you see

What your unrequited love does to me.

I know the man before me hurt you

And you'll always carry that pain with you.

But maybe there's a place in your heart for me,

A tiny nook with passion I can free.

I hope, in this niche, my love can seed.

And eventually spread and free

Your heart, which aches for all to see.

Maybe, someday you'll love me.

But, if not, loving you is enough for me.

Because, only with you, does my soul feel free.

Oh, what's the use! The man you love isn't me.

You'll always love him, and him I'll never be.

One Has My Heart

One has my heart,

The other has my name.

One I cannot leave,

While the other sulks in shame.

When she who has my name

Finds out about the other,

Will her love I lose?

Will she seek another?

The other has my heart

And knows its fragile state.

She plays an active part

In passion's anxious fate.

She's been silent in life's shadows,

Waiting the respect due.

But will her maudlin soul cry out,

and cause mine to cry out too?

Is it because I cannot choose,

Knowing the other I will lose?

Or am I just a ditherer,

Who cannot choose between two?

If I cannot juggle two loves,

Can I live with none?

These questions dog my soul,

While around my mind they run.

I stand in passion's doorway

Knowing one side I must choose,

All the while, my juggling heart

Fears which side it will lose.

I know I can't survive

In my two-loved world.

Something must give,

Or our three lives will unfurl.

A Bed Half-Full

A half-full bed and an empty chair

Reminds me that my mate is not there.

I struggled through my days of loss

And friends helped me through times of chaos.

Sometimes when I am lonely,

I remember the mellow times we had.

I will never lose my memories of her,

And they never make me sad.

Lingering decades of her love

Stay with me and rise above

The muffled din of single life

And my days of emotional strife.

My half-full bed still seems empty

Because her flesh I cannot feel,

But she comforts me in dreams.

And, in them, her love is real.

Book Section on Self-Reflection

My Place for Loneliness

There's a place I go for loneliness

That no one knows but me.

I go there only when I'm sad

To let my soul run free.

It's not a place to sulk and hide,

But it often shelters me.

I use it to regain my pride

And set my passions free.

It's not a place that others go

To relax and unwind,

Because this place I cherish so

Is deep inside my mind.

Introspection

Introspection can cloud your mind

With things you thought that you'd left behind.

When you try to unravel your sense of being,

You'll quickly see what others are seeing.

Sometimes it's good and sometimes it's bad.

But dwelling on it will drive you mad.

So, before you turn your eyes around,

Make sure your mind's on stable ground.

Sometimes

Sometimes, we let bad memories out

And keep the good ones in.

Sometimes, we dwell in fear and doubt

While we live in sin.

Sometimes, we stay above life's frays,

Although we know their cause.

Sometimes, we recognize true love,

Which makes us stop and pause.

Sometimes, we think that holding hands

Is all that love's about.

Sometimes, we feel our wedding bands

Will never let us out.

Sometimes, we think our chained souls

Are impossible to free.

Sometimes, we feel our mind is framed

By feelings we perceive.

Sometimes, we leave life's path

And wander far astray.

Sometimes, we feel fate's wrath

In subtle simple ways.

Sometimes, we've said bad things

We knew we should not say.

Sometimes, we've done bad things

That we've regretted until this day.

Sometimes, we feel death's touch

In ways we can't discuss.

Sometimes, we feel death hurts so much

It shows in all of us.

Sometimes, we felt death was much too near

While burying the dead.

Sometimes, we found that single tears

Were all our hearts could shed.

Sometimes, life is demanding,

And it causes us dismay.

Sometimes, our understanding fails us

In many ways.

Sometimes, we've learned that

'Always and *'never'* don't allow for change.

But we must learn from our mistakes,

Or our lives will never change.

Born By Death

I am my father's son,

But I did not know him,

Until he died.

I am my father's son,

But I did not miss him,

Until he died.

I am my father's son,

But I did not know me,

Until he died.

I am my father's son,

And soon became him,

Once he died.

My father's shoes,

Have been hard to fill,

Since he died.

Death, not shoes, sometimes makes the man.

The Man in the Mirror

Into an opposing mirrored world

That is not always what it seems,

I look for a pattern near or far,

That reflects my fate and dreams.

But what I see is not me,

It is something vague and vexing,

Something mysterious, something lost,

Something so distressing--

That I step back and look away

From my reflected life's reality

Before it seizes my soul in a vice-like grip

And makes me face mortality.

Lessons of Life

As fortunes wax and wane

In life's large swells and swales,

We try to ponder and remain

The person who, in youth, prevailed.

But our youthful views have changed,

And our existing needs do not entail

What, when young, were hopes retained,

Leaving our childhood dreams still veiled.

Though life created who we are,

We, as people, made key choices

That made us follow fateful stars

While ignoring more pragmatic voices.

And while our souls did ebb and flow,

We went where we were forced to go

And searched for truths so we would know

What lies beyond fate's plan bestowed.

Fading to Infinity

If you and your other you,

(That is, how people see you)

Were waveless mirrors

Put directly facing each other

In perfect parallel,

Would other people and objects

Between them in your opposing life

Continue to reflect infinitely

Until those objects and people

Gradually fade away into

Fate's tunneling darkness

Until you cannot see them at all?

Fate's Weary Way

Most of us have been missing

The timing and purpose of life.

Though busy and occasionally reminiscing,

We blindly attack our daily strife,

And avoid the deeper meaning of living.

We take no time to hold the hands of friends,

Loving others and simply giving.

We fear to look around the bends

Of roads we never traveled boldly

And relationships we could not mend.

Slowly, lovers that we never consoled

Slipped away as their lives unraveled.

Gradually, the past melted into the present

And we started wondering how we got here

From such a tortured youth and adolescence

That tried our soul and filled us with fear.

Still, we lurch forward along our lifeline,

Which is a hard line on a muddy course,

And we hope to be the runner with the fastest

time,

Whom all cheer on until they are hoarse.

Though we remember the collateral damage

That we caused along life's long way,

We know that all the guilt we can or will imagine

Cannot force us from fate's weary way.

Ambition

Opportunity and danger bracket chance

And both are players in ambition's dance.

Fates twist off when ambition consumes

And never their normal paths resume.

Sometimes, we take chances brave and bold,

Not knowing what the tenuous future holds.

Power and greed cause life's disasters.

And slaves of ambition have these two masters.

The Price of Freedom

The price of freedom is always high,

And it must be paid in full.

The ghosts of war are always nigh,

And wartime can be cruel.

We walk a lonely tranquil path

Paved by the blood of others.

Though we're weary of our wars,

There will always be another.

My Three-Man Opera

The first man is the self I know,

Or at least I think I know him.

The second man most others know

Since he's the one I show them.

The third man is my inner soul,

But I try hard to protect him.

He plays a very crucial role,

Though most cannot perceive him.

Melodies there three achieve

But only in my mind.

And in my thoughts, I do believe

Their lyrics intertwine.

These three men play distinctive roles,

But as a chorus nobody hears them,

Yet their synchrony plays a crucial role

When my life explodes in mayhem.

My Hourglass

My life is like an hourglass

Through which pass sands of time,

And through its glass constriction,

Pour memories that are mine.

While time moves quickly forward,

My memories lag behind.

I know I cannot break this rule,

Nor are there exceptions I can find.

A photograph is captured light,

Arranged by place and time.

It shows my body's aging,

But my features usually rhyme.

I live my life in three days,

Yesterday, today and tomorrow,

Those days control my destiny,

And I won't squander them in sorrow.

I live with one foot in life,

While the other is in my grave.

So, time's a thing I cherish,

Not something I spend or save.

I can't reverse my hourglass

While my time is running out.

But I can use my last few grains

To learn what life's about.

Book Section on Passing's

The Old Beggar Woman

Her struggling gait and wrinkled face

Reflected grief for her dead mate.

She'd lost her family at great cost

Before she entered society's lost.

I passed her every day on streets

And thought she was a deadbeat.

She did not have delusions grand

And only craved a kindly hand.

She limped her way down city streets

With no one's help and nil to eat.

She had no home and widely roamed

Before she spent her nights alone.

Her shrunken frame and knotted mane

Hid the fact that she was lame.

She struggled for her every breath

And every day she cheated death.

Ghosts like her die alone

And no one hears their final moan.

They fade away like apparitions,

Victims of Man's blindered vision.

Fallen Flowers

Gone are souls who always cared.

Gone are common memories shared.

Gone are loved ones old and young.

Gone are budding lives unsung

Announced by church bells too soon rung.

We all lament the friends we've lost

Once death's threshold has been crossed.

Where graveside weeping willows embower,

We cry like them for fallen flowers.

How Much Land?

Land signifies wealth and success

And wars have been fought for its defense.

To own land, people work and save,

And their holdings are envied.

But ultimately, a simple eight-foot grave

Is all that they will ever need.

Gone, But Not Forgotten

There's an atmosphere of peacefulness,

Beside each graveyard tombstone.

Remembrance, not emptiness,

Souls freed, but not alone.

Fading visions of their being,

Lost now to life's past,

Remind us that our life and living,

Are things that will not last.

Silently we ford the fog,

Of emptiness from loss.

Always forward do we slog,

No matter what the cost.

Another day, as they say,

Moves us further down life's road.

Memories fade, but still remain,

Which helps to ease our load.

Relationships we can't replace.

But still, we must adjust,

To the realities that we must face

Once dust returns to dust.

The Silent Crib

Long the silence in his crib

Where happiness once bloomed.

Draped in black are closed white doors

Of his empty nursery room.

No longer does his hobby horse

Rock wildly with abandon.

No longer does his happy voice

Echo down the hallway canyon.

Long are the faces of his parents

In the nearby silent bedroom,

Which hide unanswered questions

Among sorrow guilt and gloom.

Why does God take such good young boys

And leave their homes so unreconciled?

Nothing empties your life so quickly

As the death of your only child.

Her Wedding Day

This poem is based upon an entry in the mid-19th Century

autobiography of Theodore Clapp, an ordained Presbyterian

minister who lived for several decades in New Orleans,

Louisiana.

Of the many young brides who I've married,

None were more exquisite than her.

Her pleasant charm, and smile so merry,

Both made my old heart stir.

Her fiancé loved her deeply

And she cherished him like no other.

Her father gave her away happily,

In front of her joyful mother.

In the afternoon wedding her vows were said,

While a bouquet in hand she carried.

Their reception next was well-attended,

like many young couples that I have married.

A few hours later, she fell deathly ill.

Then suddenly, she no longer stirred.

Later that night, in her wedding dress still,

And with bouquet in hand, she was interred.

Deep within her family sepulcher

Remain four questions unanswered.

Why her? Why then?

What purpose was served?

And how does one assuage the ones who loved

her?

No Time to Say Goodbye

She slowly began to slip away,

Then suddenly she was gone.

At 1:00 am she could not stay

And died hours before dawn.

She died too fast for me to say,

"Please stay, don't move on."

And other things I never said,

Haunt me and linger on.

Where she went, I cannot follow,

And no one I know came back.

My rattled mind rings sadly hollow,

And my conscience is on guilt's rack.

She always knew she had my heart,

Yet she still wanted my soul.

Maybe I should have given in,

Because life sharing was our goal.

People hide behind life's walls

And rarely venture out.

There upon the ground they fall

And dwell among their doubts.

Silently they ask themselves,

"Why can't my soul be free?

To live my life and in love delve,

For all the world to see."

Love comes from the inside out,

It's not lightning from the blue.

And with love there are always doubts,

But it's purity we pursue.

I've kept these things all bottled up,

Between my fears and doubts.

And these things my life disrupts

Since I have never let them out.

Her sudden death I now accept

As her sad, but finite, fate.

And, at love, I'm still inept

Because my caring is second rate.

But one thing still besets my mind,

And it makes my conscience cry.

I never bothered to take the time

To prepare for her goodbye.

I will see what the future brings

Now that she has passed on.

But I cannot forget the many things

Not said that linger on.

The Tear-Stained Thread of Life

Klotho spins the thread of life,

And *Lachesis* decides its length.

Then, *Atropos* cuts the thread of life

When the time arrives for death.

Each widower has his Eurydice

Whom he longs for once she's gone.

And, like Orpheus, he craves to see

His soul-mate who passed on.

Widowers play such tearful songs,

On their soul's sad weeping lyre,

Trying to right where fate went wrong,

While still drowning in desire.

In their dreams, they see their loves

(Be them dreams by day or night).

But they find that reminiscing too much,

Only intensifies their plight.

Our minds are Gates to the Underworld

That separates ghosts from living souls.

And men must keep their emotions furled,

Once *Atropos* exacts her toll.

Men must adjust to their living world

And approach life with resolve.

Because, deep in *The Fate's* tripartite world,

There are mysteries none can solve.

Lambent Embers

I am in my life's October,

Where passion plays its role

And when embers of my memory stir,

Their sparks engulf me whole.

They help me to remember

And soothe my bereaved soul.

Mellow memories imbue my life.

And I will never let them go.

Her love embraces me like lambskin gloves.

Oh God! I miss her so…I miss her so.

Why Fate takes ones that I love,

I'll never, never know.

Why did she have to go,

Leaving my soul strewn with strife?

She haunts me so. . . She haunts me so.

Though wounded, I'm still alive.

And, like Orpheus, longing for his lost love

Memory's embers keep it alive.

She was much more than a wife

When her soul left me behind.

I'm wandering through our former life,

And among its memories, I'm trying to find,

A way forward through my forlorn life

That can mend my grieving mind.

Then again, maybe she never really left,

But became the better part of me.

Maybe she's soothing my soul,

Though still bereft,

And trying to heal my heart for me.

Take her away, and all that's left,

Is the shell of a man that others see.

Memories of her, like tender tears,

Soothe my soul on dour days,

And when life seems bleak and full of fears,

She tenderly lifts me above life's fray.

And like lambent embers not drowned by tears,

She stays. . .and stays. . .and stays.

Missing Her

I miss her mesmerizing voice

And how she cried with joy at dawn.

Her gentle smiles made me rejoice

And I hope her soul lingers on.

I miss the foolish things she did

On rainy days when stuck inside.

I miss the little girl amid

The sultry woman so wide-eyed.

I miss the times we laughed at life,

Between the days that challenged us.

Her presence helped me to survive

And made other things superfluous.

As I mingle with our memories

I can't believe that she is gone.

Her memory gives me reveries

As her soul lingers on and on.

The Golgotha Detail

Back they came at nightfall,

After a hot and grueling day,

And few words were said by all,

Though each had much to say.

Finally, the centurion said,

"I think I need a drink.

Now that rabbi's dead,

Of him, I must not think."

"I'm with that," another soldier said,

"There's a tavern down the street.

It's time to dismiss the dead,

And any secrets they may keep."

"I'll go, too" said a third one

While clutching the rabbi's robe,

"Right now, I need some well-earned fun,

Rather than some Nazarene's clothes."

So, the soldiers walked on down the street

And entered an open tavern.

But one remained near its entrance,

To guard it for his turn.

Looking at the door he openly mused,

"BY JUPITER, CAN WE N EVER DRINK IN

PEACE!

Until those pesky Zealots are dead,

I will never feel at ease."

Another soldier proposed a toast,

To the longevity of Rome.

(Legionaries always drank the most,

When they thought about their home.)

But the Centurion just kept looking down

And did not raise his glass.

His countenance carried a worried frown,

As though Fate's dice had been cast.

"His eyes," he said with candor,

"His eyes I'll never forget.

They had no hate or fear,

They had no last regrets.

And, who looks up toward the sky

And cries out for his father,

Especially knowing that he's about to die,

In the manner in which he suffered?

And, what kind of man forgives his killers,

When death from them he gets?

What purpose served his miserable death?

What Roman goal was met?"

"We weren't his only killers," said another,

After quaffing a cup of wine.

"In Rome's wars, we're all brothers,

Two more drinks and you'll be fine."

Still looking down, the centurion said,"

But the Jews were HIS brothers,

And because of them he's dead.

He was NOT LIKE all the others."

"Why not?" retorted the quaffer,

As his cup was refilled with wine.

"We're merely Pilot's enforcers," he said with

laughter,"There's no need for you to whine."

Letting out a sigh, he continued,

"Look, I'm not proud of what we've done.

In fact, like you, I feel used,

And wonder what political point was won.

But these Jews they have no honor,

They're unlike us in many ways.

They look for demons around each corner

And ramble on about their 'end of days'."

Then said the Roman centurion,

(As though to have his final say),

"But why did Pilot crucify him,

After scourging him the same day?"

"Because he would not recant his teachings,"

The legionnaire near the door said,

"And obviously, he learned nothing from his

scourging.

THAT is why he's dead."

"I was at the condemned man's side," said

another, "And heard all that Pilot said.

And I was there when the Jew was tried

And was told he would be dead.

And, what's the purpose of some silly kingdom,

In which one has to die to enter?

All we have is this life right now,

Not some…some, 'Elysian Fields for

dissenters.'

And, if this man was beloved by his God,

Then why did his God not rescue him?

What kind of ungrateful miserable God,

Leaves His favorite son to a death so grim?"

But the centurion just kept looking down

Until he received a revelation.

"Maybe, that was the whole point," he said,

"Of that condemned man's situation."

The soldiers drank on through the night,

Forgetting how their day began.

But the troubled centurion did not feel right

Fearing he had killed the Son of Man.

The Unkept Grave

At the edge of the old cemetery,

I found an unkept grave.

It was though the person interned there

Had a soul no one could save.

Her tombstone contained two dates

That showed the term of her long life.

But few remember what she was like

Before she passed on to the afterlife.

Rumors among the city old folk,

Suggested she always lived alone,

In a mansion down on Mason Road,

Where only vandals roam.

Some people say she was a spinster,

Who led a vacuous life,

And the grave's condition fit her,

Because her life was full of strife.

And others say she had two children,

Who grew up and moved away.

Those people did not know why they left,

Only that they did not stay.

So, I went to her ramshackle home,

Still vacant to this day,

And walked around its exterior

But decided not to stay.

I saw a small blank gravestone in its backyard

in an advanced stage of decay.

Some people say it marked her miscarriage,

From a lover who did not stay.

Others say it was her pet's grave,

One she loved so very much.

They couldn't remember its name,

But said it was her emotional crutch.

A few days later, I went to her grave,

And hacked down its overgrowth,

Then straightened up her tombstone,

And hoped she'd appreciated both.

But they widened the cemetery road one day

And moved her grave somewhere far away.

Nobody came forward to complain.

I found that out the other day.

Some people's lives are mysteries.

Many leave no legacy.

And like the dead buried at sea

They leave only unkept memories.